All For Love

All for Love
©2022 Maralyn Ballantyne

Published by **Hobo Jungle Press**
St. Vincent & the Grenadines, W.I.
Sharon, Connecticut, USA

First edition
February 2022

Printed in the United States of America

ISBN # 978-1-7331321-6-9
Library of Congress Control Number: 2022931480

All rights reserved. No part of this publication may be reproduced, distributed, or transmitted in any form or by any means, including photocopying, recording, or other electronic or mechanical methods, without the prior written permission of the publisher, except in the case of brief quotations embodied in critical reviews and certain other noncommercial uses permitted by copyright law.

All For Love

Maralyn Ballantyne

Contents

Preface	ix
Photos	1
Dark Chocolate Truffles	2
Not an Argument but an Experience...	3
Celebrate Me Now	4
Prince	6
Joy!	7
Absence of Words	8
No Need to Beckon	9
Love Challenge	10
Quest	11
Half an Empanada, but All of You	12
No Clark Gable, but a Darling Nevertheless	13
At the Party	14
I Found Love	15
Together We Are	16
Silence Is Golden	17
Pleasing the One You Love	18
The Perfect Thank You	19
Your Smile Belongs to Me	20
Good Morning Boo!	21
Just Be	22
Disco Ball	23
Online Dating	24
The Photo Album In My Mind	25
Memories Indestructible	26
The Meeting	28
Symbiotic Bond	29

The Couple	30
Two Minds Merge	31
Ambling Along Sterling Road	32
Love Box	33
Satisfying Find	34
Gift of Instant Recall	35
No Blue Nun, Only You!	36
A Friend Turns 81	38
Mind as Film, Poem as Photo, Word as Truth	40
Contentment	42
Fancy That!	43
Untitled	44
I Only Have Eyes for You	45
Sunshine Lover	46
After the Lunch Break	47
Seduction	48
Youthful Exuberance	49
A Thought	50
I Feel Love	51
Issues	52
Love in Moderation	53
Mother	54
Faithful Bird	55
Dear Radar	56
Lucky!	58
All Over Again	60
Pandemic Love	61
Acknowledgements	63

I dedicate *All For Love to* my daughter,
Melissa Fredericka Ballantyne

Preface

My friend, the late Audre Lorde, a poet, reminds that poetry is not a luxury but it is a vital necessity of our existence. Poetry forms the quality of the light within which we predicate our hopes and dreams toward survival and change. Anyone who knows how to love, or to suffer, or to think, anyone who wishes to live fully, needs and seeks poetry. Unfortunately, poetry remains woefully underutilized and underestimated as a medium in modern culture.

As Joan Didion, the recently departed novelist said, "All I knew (then) was what I wasn't, and it took me some years to discover what I was." In recent years I, too, have discovered what I am: a poet. Today, my most absorbed and passionate hours are spent arranging words on paper.

Join me as I take you, my readers, on an exciting journey—at times profound, at times surprising. Nowhere in *All for Love* do I ever try to explain love or to define love. I write what I feel inside of me. I feel a great deal.

Poetry writing provides the poet with relief, takes the poet out of bondage. You, as readers, are provided with comfort. Poetry gives rhythm to silence, light to darkness.

My readers, I want you to experience love and to practice acts of love through reading and digesting these poems. May *All for Love* awaken readers to the essential role love plays in human life, be it love of country, love of the environment, love of neighbor, love of foreigner, love of self, love of animal, love of deity, love of creator.

To quote William Butler Yeats (in *Where My Books Go*)
>...all the words that I write,
>Must spread out their wings untiring,
>And never rest in their flight,
>Till they come where your sad, sad heart is,
>And sing to you in the night...

Here are my poems, I leave you to do with them whatever you will.

Maralyn Ballantyne
February 2022

1. Photos

Tattered album of old photos

Vibrant memories and mottos
Fill me with love's positive impression
Familiar body language and expression
Viewing photos in the pandemic
Avoiding depression

Photos
Like colourful celebration balloons
Embracing freedom in the air
Venturing high
Moving without a care
Delighting
Triggering a tear

Sitting with the album alone
Acknowledging I will never hear your voice again on the phone
Never again will I connect with that engaging humourous tone
Nor hear you repeat you were not put on earth to turn to stone

These photos inhabit my mind
Making it their secure home

Maralyn Ballantyne

2. Dark Chocolate Truffles

Three chocolate truffles for my king
Is what I chose to bring
For him to savour while I sing.

He thanks me graciously
In him I clearly see
Beauty and sweetness of the honey bee.

Three dark chocolate truffles—a simple gift
Will give my true love a special lift
And keep him focused—may he never drift!

3. Not an Argument, But an Experience...

...and you both bring to the table your Individual Temperaments
Preconceived Notions, Hopes and Ideals.
A full menu of offerings is laid out.

Choices must be made,
A process requiring care and thought.
Don't rush into it like a mad dog.
Above all, may peace prevail.

Relationship coaches say,
Be sure he values you and shows it.
You have duties too!
It is a partnership,
A joint endeavour.
Let it be steeped in the elixir of love,
For without love, no blossoms will emerge,
No fruit will appear.

Unconditional love
Asks nothing in return.
Love freely given,
Love freely received.

4. Celebrate Me Now

Celebrate me while I breathe
Hold my hand
Show admiration
Deny me no pleasure
Tell me you love me
Look me in the eye
While I behold your image
Put red roses in my hand now
Not on my grave
Wait not for tomorrow

Converse with me
While my faculties function
While my speech is clear
While my voice is strong
While my organs operate
While my blood flows and pumps

While my heart beats
While there is pulse

Tomorrow is not promised
Not to Kings
Not to Queens
Not to those in servitude
Not even fools wait for tomorrow

Ponder on the active multi-generational community of blackbirds
Poised on the electric wires on Ives Dairy Road
A daily spectacle indeed
They harmoniously congregate to converse

To praise and celebrate each other as a way of life
Hear their melodious symphony
As they tweet in flawless unison
Effortlessly flying
A well-organized A-Team, assuming a teaching role
By example they teach the population life lessons
Willing Samaritans
Faithful sages indeed

Today is ours to hold
A delivered gift
Unwrap it now
Tomorrow may never come

5. Prince

Breezy afternoon ambling along
Head shaking
Humming a pop song
Happy to know work is done
Wondering when a Prince will come
Thinking how lucky some girls are
Thinking it is wise to aim for a star

Would he be wealthy
Would he be poor?
Would he be helpful and open the door?
Would he be well-dressed and debonair?
Would he show that he really does care?
Would he be bothered about make-up and hair?

Would he bring chocolates and roses—a special gift?
Would a prince show true love and never drift?
Would a prince have mutual interests, be patient and kind?

Would he walk through perfumed secret gardens
    in pursuit of pleasure
Hands and hearts entwined
Boundaries
Expectations
Ethics and standards defined?

6. Joy!

You bring me joy!
Pure and simple
Your expanding smile
Your pillow-talk eyes

You bring me joy!
Intense, intoxicating

You bring me joy!
Every day and every night
Your speechless testimony
Your silent story.

You bring me joy!

7. Absence of Words

Words are not your forte.
You receive me with your twinkling eyes,
You receive me with your naked smile of approval.
Words do not come easy.

Absence of words; no loss.
No loss for me; no loss for you.
The language of love soars beyond words.

Love is pure,
Love is true.
One knows when love is present.
You know that.
And so do I.

8. No Need to Beckon

Dinner digested, I headed to the sink,
I glanced back; I saw him wink.
"Oh, you look so fetching!" he uttered,
Without much ado, he beckoned.
Here was a man who acted whenever desire made its entrance.
He knew how to initiate a loving advance.
"Leave the dishes, sit here with me."
His motives were easy to see.
We savoured the moment indeed.
Today, there is little difference.
The years have not reduced his effervescence.
When he speaks to me, I escape into his world,
   buoyed by his inviting aura.
No need to beckon; I loved him yesterday, today
   and will love him tomorrow.

9. Love Challenge

To hold on or let go
To go high or go low
To make unending sacrifices
To go the extra mile every time
Wearing a brilliant smile
What to do
What not to do
When in love
This age-old question
Requires at least a suggestion
It plagues lovers everywhere
As they seek a solution
To a bad situation
What to do
What not to do
When in love
Follow the sage
You will not regret
Far would you be from the strive and the fret Pure love asks nothing in return.
And remember: no pain, no gain.

10. Quest

Don't expect me to be at your beck and call.
Don't push me; I may fall.
Don't be angry if I don't return a call.
Just be kind, value me, help me to stand tall. Together we will build a bridge (not a barrier wall) And create memories worthy of recall
As we find meaning in nature's scenes that enthrall. Let us contemplate the majesty of mountains
While throwing coins in fountains.
Let us look to the clouds as they decorate the skies Let us support each other and invigorate our ties.
Time waits on no one.
Let us act wisely and pass the test,
Showing abundant gratitude upon completing our quest.

11. Half an Empanada, But All of You

Una Mezza Porzione
You gave me half of your empanada
It was wholesome and very tasty too
Thank you my darling
But do remember that I want all of you!

I am your Queen and you are my King
I am grateful for all of the joy you bring
As we grow closer and closer day by day
Our love-bond tightens in a special way
I am thrilled that you are very handsome
Kind and thoughtful too
I look forward to sweet kisses and all of you!

12. No Clark Gable, But a Darling Nevertheless

Clark Gable, the true gentleman of the day,
   offered Vivienne a handkerchief!
How beautiful she must have felt.
So when my modern lover threw tissues at me
   as the tears poured forth
Smudging my make-up, further bruising
   my already damaged soul,
I had no option but to feel compensated
   by the tenderness in his eyes.
No handkerchief, but a caring look few can count on.

It was the last day in the office.
I was no longer going to be working alongside my twin flame.
It brought on an ocean of tears.

My darling, you mean more to me than your hankie.
Sometimes one has to put aside notions of
   old-fashioned romance and move with the times.

13. At the Party

When you are together with me at the party,
I never want the party to end.
Even when there's business to which you must attend,
   we merge in dance,
     we haunt each other in song.

Your love is King.
Pure joy you bring.

Envelop me with your strong arms.
Whisper honeyed nothings in my ear.
Move your fingers gently through my hair.
Promise that we will continue to live in harmony,
   the perfect pair.
Show me good intentions,
   how much you sincerely care.

Pause.

Be quiet now.
Deep peace.
Sweet calm.
I feel your penetrating love.
A healing aromatic balm,
Instant cure, no harm.
Words can never deliver justice
To the emotional comfort of your presence
As we effortlessly align.
Perhaps by divine design.
Like weightless ballerinas
We master all points and turns
Float with freedom
Never wanting to confine.
Stay with me at the party my darling.
May the party know no end.

14. I Found Love

I found love when it was least expected
Or perhaps love found me by surprise
Fearing for years that somehow I might be rejected
On one auspicious day, a dapper suitor did arrive
More than sheer bliss he brought along
Laughter, joy, compassion, grace
Telling me that in his heart I did belong
He bent his head and gently stroked my face
In total rapture I stood
A torrent of tears
Amazed, amazed
At last at last I found the holy grail
I prayed to God the special experience would never be erased
Our ship would be trustworthy and we would smoothly sail Find safe harbours and anchor in most exciting destinations, Where our love would thrive beyond all expectations.

15. Together We Are

An evening with my darling is very precious—it's gold.
He relates his incredible stories—words of wisdom unfold.
Like perfumed velvet rose petals lying gently in a crystal dish,
His whispers and suggestive glances deliver my special wish.
Each meeting with my true love confirms what I observed from the start,
His intentions mirror my intentions—they leap straight from the heart.

16. Silence is Golden

Sitting in brilliant sunshine or fumbling in the dark
Silence is golden you often remark.

You say it when you hear our pet dog bark
Or even when I sing an aria trying to echo like a lark.

I know you don't dislike my voice
It's simply a matter of personal choice.

So happily I comply
Never moan, never cry.

I never complain nor do I sigh
I certainly never ask you why

I look into your eyes and get the explanation
No need for direct verbal communication.

We are a loving couple, practicing silence is golden
While engaging in meditation.

17. Pleasing the One You Love

Pleasing the one you love, a never-ending exercise
Perfected by those who are not afraid to compromise
Involving duty, responsibility
Perhaps in a sense, obligation
But never indignation.
Patience, understanding
It is a feat outstanding
Fortunate are those who master the art
Bringing together the brain and the heart
What good is the one without the other
To love and be loved is not to flounder.
A kiss is not a kiss unless planted with good intention
And do not forget the three little words you should mention.

18. The Perfect Thank You

Hammered parchment would have been impressive
The words Thank You embossed with gold lettering

Using a fountain pen to write a special missive
Would have provided a gem worth preserving
Especially as I adore fine penmanship

But from the start of our relationship
It was the way your eyes conversed
No need to practice and rehearse.
Your movements were seductive
Such allure.

As you left me and made your exit
You gazed at me and from your pretty curved lips
Fluttered two little words *Thank You*
The perfect fit.

Like tasting vintage wine
I savoured the long finish
After some sips.

19. Your Smile Belongs to Me

Fleeting moments
Short and sweet
Deeply treasured
Labeled precious
Stacked with care
For easy reference
Their shelf-life automatically extended
You are here now
Yet in a flash you could be gone
In my dreams
In my imagination
Your smile belongs to me
Held in place
Yesterday
Today
Tomorrow
Forever

20. Good Morning Boo!

Good Morning Boo!
One look at you and I know it is not your finest hour.
Your face looks sour.
You are not in fine fettle.
It will take some time before you settle.
Be kind and helpful; put on the kettle.
We'll sip cups of English Breakfast tea.
Relax Boo, count on me, love is the key.
We'll chat; if we get lucky, we'll see eye to eye.
Don't even ask; it is too early for a slice of key lime pie. You asked me to be patient with you,
That I'll be; I'll be attentive, too.
You reminded me that you are not a talker,
And you do not want me to be your stalker.
But listen my friend, I am not your unpaid social worker. I'll help you reason,
Explain that everything has its season;
But you must make efforts to be positive,
Out the window must go the negative.

21. Just Be

When the song *Just the Way You Are* became a hit
I told myself I will just be

And so I have always been me
Never trying to be someone else

Now that we are together,
I find myself telling you just be
That is the key.

Follow the mantra—just be and be free
Your true persona will shine bright
You will radiate light
Just be
Just be

22. Disco Ball

Here I come, your big bright disco ball.
Join me; listen to our beloved songs.
Let us heal the world's wrongs.
How much better does life get my love?
Mimic the peace dove.
Music is a blessing from above.
Feed on my fun-loving energy,
Make it a top priority.
Make it your ideology.
Today—Nature Boy by Grady Tate.
The greatest thing you'll ever learn,
Is just to love and be loved in return.

23. Online Dating

No waiting.
Find the one you are seeking.
Hopefully it is the one you will be keeping!
High success rates on matching.
Download the app,
And very quickly a new lover is in your lap.
No long talking, no crap.
You don't need a road map.
Browse and take a nap.
Online dating, a short rap.
Make it a cool and flirty chat.
Be savvy as you interact.
Ask leading questions
Before making selections,
And soon you know where it's at.
It's online dating,
A new way of relating
Without too much debating.
A new way of mating.
Read the high rating.

24. The Photo Album in My Mind

No need to go to the computer to download
In my mind the images will sequentially unfold
Engraved on my heart
Exclusively mine to hold.

No need to look through the filing cabinet
To find the notes about the day we met
Everything is now part of my DNA
Details are not forgotten yet

No need to consult the journal to find out what we did in May,
It is crystal clear in my mind
We celebrated your birthday.

The images and details are easy to find
Etched in gold leaf on the vellum of my mind
Everything recorded
Archived from the start
Artistically presented
Engraved on my heart.
Each image
Each moment
Each scenario an important part

Laden are the drawers and shelves of my soul
Like a full-fledged orchestra each image plays a role.
Invisible kisses swirl around my neck and my face,
Moving in unison with me at my gentle pace
Like an artist you trace your fingers over my eyes

Your love and affection radiate wherever I go
From place to place.

25. Memories Indestructible

I remember that moment when I saw smoke consuming
   our backyard;
It was my mother working hard.
She said she was getting rid of useless papers; cleaning.
There I was, disgruntled and dreaming.
She was burning the box of love letters you penned to me
   many moons ago,
Treasures I planned to cling to, never to let go.
I remember feeling gutted upon finding love poems
   in a garbage bin, poems I birthed to you,
Tossed there by my sister who was cleaning, too!
I remember my utter anguish
When my beloved son accidentally trashed memorabilia
   related to our courtship.
He too, was cleaning!

Today, my love, I too am cleaning;
Clearing cobwebs from the windows,
   doors and corridors of my mind.
All compartments are neat and in order;
Nothing to toss nor trash did I find.
The captured memories in my mind are completely in place
Indestructible,
Neatly stacked, chronologically filed
Indelible.

How joyful to dwell amongst love letters, dried flowers
   and mental images you bestowed upon me,
What comfort, solace, nourishment and gratitude
   for perfect physical and mental vision.
I delight in the happy past,
Though material does not forever last.

Loss is part of the journey.
It is the destination that counts—eternity.
Though we cannot see each other's face
(You having ended the race),
We are enjoined in a happy place
In sweet communion
In wholesome fellowship,
Members of the same fraternity.

As the material disintegrates and enters the ecosystem, I turn attention to the Holy Trinity.

26. The Meeting

A tear for the meeting
A tear for the greeting
A tear for the parting
Perhaps a new love affair is starting

You gave me your hand
I gave you my heart
Your words were few
As we savoured the brew
You spoke with your eyes
You never told lies
We knew we were reaping
Rich harvest for keeping

A kiss for the meeting
A kiss for the greeting
A kiss for the parting
As we witness a new life worth charting

It is never too late
We know not our fate
Life is about living
Sharing and giving
You gave me your hand
I gave you my heart
We bonded
Your words I will forever treasure
Thank you for the intimacy
An overwhelming gesture
Thank you for the intense pleasure

27. Symbiotic Bond

As we greet sunrise each morning, as we salute the moon
 when our toil is finished,
I focus on our symbiotic bond and pray that we will
 always be replenished.
You, my love, embody high intellect, poise, grace,
Vulnerability, sensitivity, emotional balance and imbalance,
 the total human face.
Go gently, walk the walk and dance the dance of the universe
 at your own pace.
Partake of the pie of life, drink from the fountain of youth,
 and positivity embrace.
Loving each other intensely is what we master
 with great perfection.
May our unique liaison continue to deliver perpetual joy
 and satisfying reflection.
On our journey together, we will continue to collect
 experiences rich and rewarding.
We will worship God, favour primordial simplicity
 and never be over demanding.
We will store dreams for de-dreaming and relate
 mysterious stories.
Every cell in my body will remember you
 and should I become lost in the forest of memories,
You will be there, my faithful compass,
 helping me to navigate,
To find center, retrace, move forward, energize
 and invigorate.

28. The Couple

Tickle me with a feather
Shield me from stormy weather
Let us break a wish bone
Taste my ice cream cone
Check out a sexy photo of you on my phone
Life is dynamic
Not cast in stone
Stay in my zone
But lower your tone
We are both under pressure
Save our bond from rupture

As we enjoy some childish things
We thank God for whatever life brings
The pretty birdie that sings
The bleeding heart vine that clings
The artistry of the butterfly's wings
Our capacity for wild imaginings
Pause for a moment
Pray
Repent
Slow down on decision-making
Avoid those who are faking
Praise God upon waking
Focus on uplifting
Greet each new day in an exceptional way
Come what may love is here to stay
This is not the time to stray
Be mindful of the words you say

We are a pair
Show love
Kindness
Care
Forget about shedding a tear
With God there is nothing to fear
As we positively welcome the new year
And think about our friends far and near

29. Two Minds Merge

Your hand outstretched in the air
Meets my outstretched hand in the air
A gesture
At a certain time
In a certain place

To the witnesses on the periphery
Their thoughts focused on the periphery
Two meet
Superficial motion
Random it seems
A meaningless happening
Chance perhaps

But it was a beginning before it even began
Governed by the infinite realm of hope
Triggering the happening after the end
Leading to convergence
The merging of two minds

30. Ambling Along Sterling Road

Tightly focused on the amorous, walking side by side
  (Not the type of walk where one reflects on the waistline
  and wants to hide, or glances frantically at a pedometer
  to make sure miles are being completed).
A silent walk in the morning on a deserted road.
A meditative walk with a loved one, hand in hand.
What did we do to deserve this?
It is as if a fairy is waving a magic wand.

Along the way, a new type of marathon runner:
An iguana in brightly coloured gear.
Then a blackbird étude, followed by chirping migratory
  birds partying overhead, pair by pair.
We pause to contemplate Mother Nature together,
Engage in light banter
Grasp the moment like there is no other.

Some live for the big moment;
Celebrations with pomp and show.
We live for sunrise:
Its constancy,
Its spiritual symbolism,
Its glow.
We absorb energy from old resilient trees,
Shy wild flower blooms peeping from crevices.

Celebrating simple pleasures,
We look into each other's eyes
Assimilating a lovebird's mating call
We have found treasures.

31. Love Box

Lazy Sunday.
No fun day.
It is the time of Covid lock-down.
Few planes fly, no one wants to go to the town.
Multi-layered headless thoughts aimlessly float around.
Colourful competing out-of-the-box ideas abound.

Endless hours in which to self-examine and reflect.
Anxiety mounting, not knowing what to expect.
Suddenly the whole world shut its doors.
Business closed on all its floors.
Face-to-face transactions a mode of the past.
Going to the office once a ritual, now dying fast.

Filling the unemployment form,
Staying at home, the new norm.
705 Radio, my faithful companion,
In awe, as I contemplate God in the exercise of dominion.
What will I do today?
I will follow protocols in every way.

Wear my mask.
Complete a household task.
Hug a tree,
And just be!
Here comes the beloved St. Vincent Love Box,
Cornucopia of fresh local Vincy fruits and vegetables with which to nourish and detox.

32. Satisfying Find

No immediate wow moment punctuated by thrills,
No charcoal fringes competing with fluffy gold frills.
No dusty oranges and fiery reds almost touching the hills.
I looked deeper, just a little deeper,
In awe of our Saviour, the keeper,
Uncovering layers of marshmallow pink and pearly fuchsia,
A subtle spilling of secrets of the universe,
Rewarding my sky search,
While reclining on my hammock perch.
Poking around the sky,
Then hovering around the psyche of my friend, now up high,
And re-discovering a beautiful mind,
Re-calling acts compassionate and kind.
Not surprising, this outstanding two-fold satisfying find!

33. Gift of Instant Recall

The photographs of her you carry around in your mind's eye
Will remain with you until you die.
That you can no longer see her face,
No longer pen a love note, doodle or trace,
Should not cause you to cry,
Or even trigger a sigh.
Place your eyes in the direction of the sky.
Think of her fetching features
The music and choreography created as birds tweet and fly,
The perpetual wonders up high.
Focus on exchanging exciting stories that mutually enthrall.
Run with the ball.
Focus on the priceless gift of instant recall.
Leave your message of gratitude indelibly inked on the wall.

34. No Blue Nun, Only You!

Your choice of wine was nothing to write home about;
   your intellect was your crown,
You the Rhodes scholar, Oxford educated, with salt
   of the earth roots anchored in Jamaica's Irish Town.
Me, friend of Madame Lalou Bize-Leroy and the DRC,*
   responded to your Blue Nun with a frown;
But it mattered not, for in you I unearthed treasures untold.
Every nanosecond in your company was mine to claim
   and forever hold,
At least, so I felt for a long time, until a surprising story
   did unfold.
Difference in wine preference was insignificant.
My lenses zoomed in on the long haul: a life together
   in harmony
Healthy, happy, abundant.

Your goddess, your forever princess, greets you today,
Not with wine, but with a steady outpouring of sentiments,
   rose petals strewn on the pathway.
Here are the words and thoughts that remained buried in me
   for decades
Allow me to present them now, lest memory fades:
The thrill of listening to the BBC's Alistair Cooke's
   Letter from America on the colonial Georgetown verandah,
We both riveted, focusing on geo-politics
   (no time for our minds to wander)
Your high-performance battery-powered Phillips radio
   so impressed us
That you, in your usual calming and generous manner,
   gifted me one without a fuss!

You, unaware of the way my eyes always walked all over you
As I reflected on the lyrics to *Something*
(Something in the way he moves attracts me
   like no other lover).

Too shy was I to utter sensual words in your ear,
But willing to bear onerous loss and pain,
I enveloped and consumed you in sweet silence
Over and over again.
Never could I have enough of the potential twin-flame.
Every moral you shared was mine to retain.
My actions speaking louder than words!
Here is your beloved Glenfiddich from the Scotland
   of our forebears,
And here am I, sentimental, cast in poetic model ,
   competing with Plath's *Ariel*.
Smile now my love, fear not; your past is not on trial.
It just took me a very long time to express myself,
Like grand cru burgundy that ages gracefully on the shelf
Exposing multiple layers of aromatic flavor,
Surprising nuances with the passage of time,
While existing challenges, impediments, reasons
   for dissatisfaction remain hard to define.
How honourable and fulfilling it feels to be true to oneself.
Salute the strong Maasai woman in my DNA,
Presenting a canvas of pleasant brush strokes in a unique way.

*Domaine de la Romanee-Conti, a famous wine estate in Burgundy, France.

35. A Friend Turns 81

Armchair travel elevated itself, topping the half empty agenda.
No more taxis to airports.
No need to check meeting dates on the calendar.
No need to be mindful of strict diplomacy.
Life now welcomes unpolished thoughts.
Pure candour.
The mind is completely free to meander
From subject to subject, to aimlessly wander,
To venture out on a frolic of its own,
To fly as high as any curious drone.
At 81, you are ruler sitting on a throne.
No demands for accountability,
Just practicing the usual civic responsibility.
No colonial uniform,
Casual wear now the norm.
Shaving and looking in the mirror three times,
An unnecessary act.
No need to sign a pact.
No need to corroborate a fact.
No competitions, no mountains to climb, no races to run;
Loads of time to relax and have fun,
To fantasize and absorb the sun.
The afternoon nap now the assured prize.
81 today; something difficult to realize.

More than ever before, you look forward to a surprise.
And here it comes; not one you may quickly surmise—
An unexpected telephone call from a beloved friend,
Stirring deep emotions but making the life-journey
   easier to comprehend;
Nothing onerous like a thesis to defend.

On this special birthday,
Drift into the golden years clutching every fleeting sun ray.
Count your blessings, be grateful and pray.
No need for a speech; much to feel, little to say.
It is about reflection on a life well-lived, an OJ*
   and doing it your way:
Gratitude, tender friendships sustained, bonds forged
   while traversing each pathway,
Insights collected, treasures unearthed, memories created
   while exploring an irresistible byway.

An eighty-first birthday is time for introspection
As much as it is a time for joyful celebration.

---

*OJ=Order of Jamaica (conferred on a Jamaican citizen of outstanding distinction).

36. Mind as Film, Poem as Photo, Word as Truth

Was there a photograph, I would place it on your plate,
But you would not be able to partake
How fortunate our times together remain indelible,
   engraved on my mind,
Thanks to my ability to capture memories in poems,
   leaving tears behind.
One pays a high price when one loves unconditionally, Opening oneself to disappointment, grief, loss,
   unending fragility.
When one is ready, the other is gone;
Both are sometimes torn.

A sleepy unfamiliar beach house on the
   West Coast of Barbados,
Almost slips gracefully into the ocean carrying us
   willingly along,
As we quickly feel at ease, as if we belong,
Like staying in our own yard.
The laughter of the two children brings the scene alive,
Competing with the crashing sound of the waves,
   the streaming of the Jackson Five.
A happy foursome oozing energy and totally exuberant,
Fueled by inviting tropical Easter weather, the sun displaying
   its brilliance.
Energetic you mastering breast strokes,
Me, content to throw my cares to the bay.
The two young ones at play, their engaging nanny
   leading the way

All for Love

Leaving us to enjoy time together (intimacy being rare
   when four prying eyes are forever in search mode,
Able to peer through every crevice, breaking through every code).
But Heaven it was; an Easter holiday in Barbados;
One worth recalling over and over again
And never in vain.
No lobbies to navigate, no phone calls to decline or take,
   no suffering at the mercy of negligent service staff,
Just free and peaceful, watching the world go by
   and having a laugh,
Far from the madding crowd, bereft of frenzy,
   in our cozy little beach cottage,
Both of us aligned on the same page.
With hindsight; it was the microcosm of the macrocosm
   that for a long time, haunted me.
Blue skies are all I could see.
I was busily building dreams; hoping to manifest
   a desired outcome.
With the passage of time, the picture changed,
   but something central remained the same:
The notion that there is no higher reward than a quiet
   minimalist life in communication with a loved one,
Ideally physically together, but physically together
   or physically apart,
It is not about head; it is all about heart!

37. Contentment

You never gave me a box wrapped and tied up with string.
For as long as I have known you,
You have never given me a thing.
But oh, what joy you daily bring!
Oh, how you set my heart on fire and make me sing.
No need to search for gifts in a closet,
(At least not yet!)
Or re-read gift tags
And count stuffed shopping bags
In order to enjoy your offering.
Your kisses have greater meaning.
I am content
Living in the moment.
I do not look up on the top shelf;
I simply look in the mirror at myself.
I look like I am in good health.
The smile you painted on my face is my wealth.

38. Fancy That!

Amidst devastation
Forest destruction
Environmental pollution
Ecological destabilisation
Continuous land erosion
Disappearance of lush vegetation
Unfolding deprivation
Entire villages stripped naked with impunity—degradation
There stands Fancy
Fancy that
Spectacular forest cover display—elegant green hat
Paths curtained with flowers, a vibrant grassy foliage mat
An assured welcome at the forest door
Birds still chirp as they realign

Fancy
Unscathed, undisturbed, pristine
God's work—an outstanding sign
Behold vista sublime
Beacon of hope
As we, the people, struggle to cope

Fancy.
Reminder of green realities,
Community love and unity, endless happy possibilities.

39. Untitled

Passage of time does not bonds break.
Amazing what an emotional high passage of time can make.
In the process, much one will leave, but much one will take.
That my eyes did not survey you for many years,
Did not close the floodgate to stop passion and joyful tears,
Did not distort any aspect of our re-visit.
The lamp of love remained lit.
Behold! The memory of the tenderness in your voice;
To live all over again, you would still be my choice.

Our lips parted in an invisible kiss.
We reconnected in bliss
Upon hearing each other through a device.
No need for verbal explanation, no need for compromise.
Passage of time is but a happening.
Something that takes place,
Sometimes producing welcome smiles on our faces,
Its impact we cannot predict,
Our reactions we do not select.
Our bonds of love, passage of time did re-kindle and resurrect;
Like pulling a drawer of a filing cabinet,
Scanning volumes of memorable details.
With the passage of time
Our relationship of trust, compassion, human kindness,
Born of destiny, nourished by the nectar of love,
   seeped in intoxicating happiness,
Resurfaced freely, its pristine beauty intact,
Wings unclipped, two fertile minds, both willing
   and ready to interact.

40. I Only Have Eyes for You

Beautiful surprising cloud formations you will not likely
  ever view again,
Spectacular sky colours you will not likely
  bear witness to again,
Nor will you revel with me under a crescent moon,
  nor see it wane.
Mother nature's subtle hues will no longer bring you private
  emotional lift and numb inner pain.
Here am I playing with them all and earnestly
  representing you!
Time for you to welcome a dimension that is absolutely new.
Now it is my turn to do something for you,
And your turn to once again do something for me, too.
Better late than never; you, suitor ready to woo.
Comforting moon rises, resolute sunsets, magical full moons,
  we experienced together.
These natural wonders still display daily
In your mind's eye you salute them, even in bad weather.
Outstanding memories abound, each one competing
  with the other.
Never mind; with my gift of vision, on your behalf
  I acknowledge them all.
I am still always watching for you, my friend,
  as you may recall.
Every time my voice greets you, you are seeing
  and participating in a Godly delight
Through a very special mode, and how your fertile
  imagination must take joyful flight.

41. Sunshine Lover

Flirting enthusiastically in your golden years,
The sun grins with you
And kisses you, too,
As you partake of the energy it radiates.
You suck up its glow,
You soak up its health benefits,
Vitamins, feel-good factor, all its merits,
Absorbed from head to toe.
Cavorting seven days in a row,
Nothing stops your party with the sun.

With the sun you walk,
With the sun you run.
When I shout,
"Fred, get out of the sun; I know it's fun."
You giggle and reply, "I love the sun!"

Should the sun go on Twitter,
Well done
Well done
Will be the tweet!

42. After the Lunch Break

The lunch break is over now,
And wow, wow!
We are still sitting here.
Another harsh word from you and I may shed a tear.
Every time you behave this way, you put me in fear.
Do not forget to listen to my voice,
We both need to reason before making a choice.
This is not about burning bras and feminism,
This is about our lives, fair play and avoiding a deeper schism. We
need to review our marriage vows and our life goals,
To re-energize, search our hearts and souls.
Remember the old saying: you reap what you sow.
Look up, here comes a promising rainbow
Outdoing the surrounding gloom.
Tonight, nature will bless us again: a rare full moon.
Let us revisit that glorious day when we became
   bride and groom.
The pandemic may not end anytime soon,
Meanwhile, we must try to cope by together
   singing the same tune.

43. Seduction

Here is a perfume bottle; *Ma Griffe* by Carven,
Which you presented, as a gift of mystery,
Telling me how sensual it smells,
As part of my body chemistry.

The art of seduction you mastered with ease,
You knew how to crack a joke,
How to tease, how to please.

You have not changed after all of these years,
Bringing me to the point of uncontrollable laughter,
To the brink of joyful tears,
Like when you wished me happy birthday
On my phone call to you,
As we celebrated your 81 years.

44. Youthful Exuberance

I hope that you do experience
The youthful exuberance
That I experience
During this endless happy journey of loving you
Tell me if you do
Tell me if you don't
I want to know

Maralyn Ballantyne

45. A Thought

A thought pure and heavenly floats on my mind,
A thought that reminds me you are loving and kind.
As you sit not far from me, immersed in your game,
I make the love connection, I repeat your name.
Today, our moments together are brief,
Though greatly treasured and true.
A full-fledged rendezvous is urgently due.

46. I Feel Love

Love—a gentle caring concern
I happily discern
Deeply ensconced in the recesses of the heart
Whose power is felt
Every minute
Every hour
Every day

Love—flowing from a sensuous embrace
As you quietly stroke and caress my face
As you repeatedly squeeze my hand
Strolling along on the powdery sand

Love—enveloping
Mind
Heart
Body
Soul
As we sing hymns and listen to church bells toll.

Feeding my hungry heart.
While we are together,
While we are apart.

47. Issues

You don't mind that I did not tattoo your name on my wrist,
Nor that wearing a bracelet with your name is not on my list.
Mum did not flaunt Dad's name,
Yet they shared 70 years of bliss.
They said I love you now and then,
Spontaneously blew a kiss.

I guess they got it right.
They knew how to avoid a fight!
They ate dinner together every night.
It was the norm at that time,
They saved every dime.

Who does such things anymore?
Do couples still discuss everything right to the core?
Many honestly feel doing so is quite a bore.
We ought to reflect on old times, Caribbean folk lore,
Bring issues in our relationship, up front, to the fore.
Without a doubt, we both know issues abound,
Let us not wake up one day to a rapidly deteriorating wound.

48. Love in Moderation

Outspoken
Kamala Harris says she is not obsessed with her Doug
He makes a great quiz partner at a pub
Her words resonate well with many and even reverberate
A friend once showed me how quickly obsessive love
　can evaporate
He and his lover scared each other off
The relationship did deteriorate
Moderation in all things say the sages
Such advice has worked well throughout the ages

Don't be too overwhelming
Possessive
Or aggressive
Tone down
Be at times passive
In small doses
Love is indeed a many splendoured thing
Intoxicating man and woman
Making them dance and sing
Elevating lovers to queens and kings

Crazy obsessive love makes lovers intensely cling
Broken promises
Pain
Much heartbreak it can bring

49. Mother

Faithful messenger, faithful friend,
One who stands tall and under pressure does not bend,
One on whom I can always depend.
Whenever there appears a crack, you immediately mend.
My word you are ready to defend.
You provide sunshine, should gloom descend.

Quick to clarify, quick to amend,
My every motive, my every intention, you comprehend.
You and I follow the same trend.
It does not matter what length message I send,
You transmit it fully from beginning to end.
There is no doubt that you are a Godsend.

With you in my life,
Peace prevails; there is no strife.
When I tire, you are ready to energize.
To enlighten and organize.
You perform your role, not expecting a prize.
I never suffer burn out because you revive.

You are Mother
Strong lifelong symbol, like no other.
Outstanding producer,
Carer, feeder, supreme giver,
Angel on earth, angel above,
You are Mother, you are unconditional love.

50. Faithful Bird

For two years you visited me every morning
  at my bathroom window
Dutifully you chirped for 730 days in a row
You shared my chocolate cookie
Then off you would go
Performing your show sweetly
Making sure I did not sink low

Never could I imagine a morning without your presence
  my faithful friend
I regarded you as the companion God to me did send
You are the type of mate I recommend
To you a warm welcome I forever extend
You, brightly coloured, light, slender,
You who did not offend
You who uplifted my spirit
Giving me a much-needed lift
Your melody became my melody
Penetrating mind, soul, body
Your sweet birdsong reverberated in my head all day long
Now I must face a life without you
Mourning you, star of the bird galaxy, is all that I do

Thanks to brilliant footage in my memory bank
I still picture you trying your silly prank
Displaying your sunny temperament
With one single foot, beak slightly bent
Showering the world with gratitude and contentment
While I cannot easily replace your unique presence, your charm,
Indelible memories of you envelop me, keep me calm

51. Dear Radar

I am reflecting on our face-to-face conversations
And various pleasant associations,
How the pandemic put spent to engaging ritual,
Normal activity, nuances and the visual,
Personal experiences not replaced by Zoom and any virtual.

Eyeball-to-eyeball, we united by physical proximity, human touch.
We both enjoy that very much.
Recall how you often pinched me on a certain part,
The outpouring of feeling, the love that gushed from your heart.
Together, we represent a major work of art!

Whether you were telling me about coffee-growing
   Blue Mountain,
Or about wishing and throwing coins in an Italian fountain,
Or playfully spilling in my ear a bag of honey-laced nothing,
Each word and even your silence, brought a special something.
Face-to-face interaction, my hand on your leg
A real outing.

One day you said how sad you felt as Cindy, love of your life,
Went off to live with Bob Marley and wished to be his wife,
And how you drove to 56 Hope Road, Kingston,
Hoping to view her face one more time, for closure
   and resolution.
Often we discussed Jamaica's environmental pollution.

Sometimes we covered your life as a US soldier stationed
   in Florence, Italy:
Italian women, extra virgin olive oil, penne arrabbiata
   and glorious gastronomy,
Your mother's ancestry in the heart of Africa,
Why you declined to accompany your English fiancée
   Lady Victoria,
To the wedding of Prince Charles and Diana Spencer.
In each face-to-face engagement,
I captured your essence, your refinement,
Your love of clean fun, crisp humour, a pun, simple entertainment,
Your penchant for lively rapport,
The way you spontaneously throw open a welcoming door.
And for those things, I am nostalgic and will adore you evermore.

52. Lucky!

I was not searching for a lover or a new male friend,
Nor was there a message or hint I was trying to send,
When I landed on you like a monarch butterfly finding milkweed.

It was a sultry Sunday afternoon
Just before the Harvest Moon,
Perfect timing, mere chance, fate, mystery.
It was the start of our expanding love story
Give God the glory!
May our joy continue forever.

Perhaps the calm aura you maintain
Keeps us productive and sane,
Helps our bond grow and sustain,
As we bear witness to sweet refrain,
Void of emotional suffering and pain.

A tight embrace,
As I feather stroke your face.
We dictate our pace.
No need for haste,
And no time to waste.

A tender kiss
Nourishing moments of shared bliss.
I never asked your intention,
The future you did not mention.
Yet neither of us experience tension.

We continue to move along aimlessly,
Waxing romantic; balmy.

All for Love

We are enjoying our journey.
We do not have much money.
We are happy whether it is rainy or sunny.

Friends say that no one lives that way,
But we continue without a care, we sway.

Living from pay cheque to pay cheque.
Not daunted by the many bills we must pay
Focusing not on tomorrow but today.

We know that love is here to stay.
Our vibrant love makes life magical,
Added to that, is our deep appreciation of the theatrical.
Immersing ourselves in some simple pleasure,
Another afternoon of unadulterated leisure.

Pausing to stand and stare
Without a care,
We do not the future fear.
True friendship is indeed becoming rare,
It is true friendship we greatly value and share.

Lucky us, the true match, the perfect pair.
Buckets overflowing with melodic laughter,
No need to shed a tear.
We both move to the music we hear.
Any obstacle we together clear,
Each other's load we jointly bear.
You, my friend, so dear.

53. All Over Again

Getting old, feeble and blind is how you describe your condition.
Your active mind and congeniality I observe with great emotion.
There you are, at a ripe eighty-one years of age,
Seated on the retirement stage
Thousands of miles away from me.
And here am I, loving you all over again, with glee.
Chances are we will not again touch each other physically,
But we are faithfully communicating digitally.
Interfacing with you in conversation after an impasse
Is satisfying, much more than I expected.
It could have been the case I found myself rejected.
As I speak with you, your sensual copper-toned skin
   is magically reflected.
Your physical energy and agility of former times
   though not easy to find,
Does not reduce the pleasure, as the focus is on the brilliance
   of your perfect mind,
Recollections of your illuminating aura and that you were
   forever kind.
I not only hear your expressive words, I feel you
   in the marrow of my bones.

One day long ago, at an airport, you,
Engrossed in a novel by John le Carre,
Sat close to me, as we awaited news regarding our flight delay,
Suddenly, you put in my hand, a bit of paper,
On it, boldly written, your private number.
These dramatic details, I'll always vividly remember
From January through December.
Before I knew it, I was not only in love with Le Carre's
   George Smiley, but madly in love with you!

54. Pandemic Love

Every day I hug myself
(A virtual hug does not help)
I try not to cry
I try to keep my spirits high

I sip my hard cider
Make myself a better writer
Remind myself of the warrior women poems I wrote
Digest the ones on spiritual growth
Revel in compliments bestowed upon my writing
Marvel at how months fly by like lightning
Look to nature for inspiration
Simple pleasures worthy of celebration

The pandemic tore many couples apart
Many now suffer a broken heart
Some cry themselves to bed like a babe
As they witness relationships slowly fade
Some lovers are stranded in different places
Not knowing if
They ever will kiss each others' faces

The pandemic closed and opened doors
Some couples will remain together bonded
Others will emerge wounded or dumbfounded

Acknowledgements

The decision to publish *All For Love* is an emotional event, if only because I remained a secret poet for a long time. Each and every poem in this collection was birthed out of real life situations and circumstances I personally faced. Whenever I got brave enough to put a few lines on my Facebook wall, my friends immediately asked for more. I therefore profusely thank all of them. Their interest encouraged me to get published.

I thank my mother who was totally fascinated with my poems and wanted to hold *All For Love* in her hands, but sadly left us before it could happen.

To my editors, Ruth Boerger and Marc Erdrich at **Hobo Jungle Press,** sincere appreciation and thanks for making the publishing process such an enjoyable journey.

I am most appreciative to all the special people in my life who listened to poems now published in *All for Love* and gave the seal of approval. My relationships with them provided context, substance and material for many of the poems.

Thanks to very early inspiration from the late Derek Walcott, Nobel Prize Winner for Literature 1992, who in various interactions with me, convinced me I had both a gift for poetry, as well as capability.

Words from Derek Walcott's 1992 Nobel Lecture come alive in *All For Love*: "Poetry conjugates both tenses simultaneously; the past and the present." and "There is buried language and there is the individual vocabulary, and the process of poetry is one of excavation and of self-discovery."

www.ingramcontent.com/pod-product-compliance
Lightning Source LLC
Chambersburg PA
CBHW020548080526
44583CB00013B/1044